PRINCE NASEEM

Lord Of The Ring

PRINCE NASEEM

Lord Of The Ring

TIM SMITH

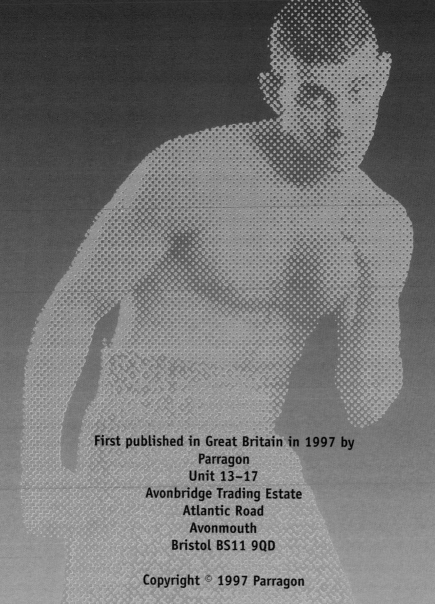

First published in Great Britain in 1997 by
Parragon
Unit 13–17
Avonbridge Trading Estate
Atlantic Road
Avonmouth
Bristol BS11 9QD

Copyright © 1997 Parragon

ISBN 0-75252-398-8

Produced by Prima Creative Services
Editor Roger Kean
Design and repro by Prima Creative Services

Printed and bound in Italy

Acknowledgements

Main cover photograph: Allsport/John Gichigi; lower cover and back cover photographs: Mark Thompson; title page photograph: Al Bello;
end page photograph: Phil Cole. Background graphics from photographs by: Allsport/Al Bello 18, 38, 47, 85; Phil Cole 1, 11, 14, 22, 27, 30,
36, 37, 52, 59, 75, 80, 93, BC; John Gichigi 1, 3, 4, 9, 20, 24, 25, 28, 29,39, 40, 43, 62, 63, 64, 67, 70, 71, 77, 83, 88, 91, BC;
Mark Thompson 10, 15, 23, 42, 56, 74

The publishers would like to thank everyone at Allsport for their kind help and support in bringing
this project to fruition at 'impossible' speed, especially Lee Martin and Mark Goldsmith...

AND TO
Prince Naseem Hamed, the annihilator – as all British boxers should be.

MARK THOMPSON: ALLSPORT

CONTENTS

INTRODUCTION ····· **6**

1992 ····· **14**

    14 Ricky Beard; 16 Shaun Norman; 18 Andrew Bloomer;

    20 'Miguel' Matthews; 22 Des Gargano; 24 Peter Buckley

1993 ····· **26**

    26 Alan Ley; 28 Kevin Jenkins; 30 Chris Clarkson

1994 ····· **32**

    35 Peter Buckley (back for more!); 36 John Miceli;

    37 Vincenzo Belcastro; 40 Antonio Picardi; 42 Freddy Cruz;

    46 Laureano Ramirez

1995 ····· **50**

    52 Armando Castro; 54 Sergio Liendo; 56 Enrique Angeles;

    58 Juan Polo-Perez; 62 Steve Robinson

1996 ····· **66**

    67 Said Lawal; 70 Daniel Alicea; 74 Manuel Medina;

    76 Remigio Molina

1997 ····· **78**

    80 Tom 'Boom Boom' Johnson; 84 Billy Hardy; 88 Juan Cabrera

PRINCELY STATS ····· **92**

Naseem Salom Ali Hamed

was born in Sheffield, South Yorkshire 23 years ago to Yemeni parents. Named 'Prince' by his trainer and mentor Brendan Ingle, and 'Naz' by the rest of the world, the man is a multiple world champion, record breaker and record maker.

He began training in Ingle's St. Thomas's gym at the ripe old age of seven years, and by the time he was 12 was already making headlines in the local press. Never one for the conventional

approach, he deviates from the norm of young high-profile sportsmen and always has. While he doesn't drink, gamble or womanise, he is also noted for sleeping in, chomping on chocolate and turning up for post-midnight training sessions.

His early years are peppered with fight after fight with bigger, more experienced men. Although he's learnt a great deal from stablemates and trainers, you can't teach the kind of raw talent and unbelievable speed that are his and his alone.

In a stroke of fatherly love that can be seen as a genius move for the boxing world, his father, Sal, took him to the gym, fearing that the slight, small lad could suffer from racist attacks and abuse. Some chance!

He was raw in the early days, but not so raw as to fool his trainers and many of his sparring partners. He's boxed for England, although he moved out of the amateur realm before he had a chance to score an Olympic gold medal – which would certainly have been his. He's won belt after belt and still the boxing world deride him for entertaining people, and bringing a new audience to the 'sweet science'. Whatever the rest of the world thinks of him, his record stands all scrutiny and he will box on.

A dad's joy: thanks to fears Naseem's father Sal had over his son suffering from racial abuse at school, Britain can now boast one of the best boxers of all time. Here, Naz and his father celebrate a successful defence of the WBO and IBF Featherweight titles after beating Argentinian Juan Cabrera in July 1997.

JOHN GICHIGI: Allsport

BRENDAN INGLE

Naz's trainer and, it must be said, mentor is a savvy Irishman by the name of Brendan Ingle. Brendan and his son, John – one of Naz's closest allies – run the St. Thomas's Boys' Club in Wincobank, a rough area just outside of Sheffield.

Born in 1930, Brendan found himself marooned in industrial Sheffield, a smoky pit of steel and coal, capital of South Yorkshire. He was 18 and just over from Ringsend, the appropriately named area in the centre of Dublin, looking to make his fortune in England. No fears for Brendan, though; he was well used to fending for himself – if only to get some breakfast in competition with the rest of his 15-strong family.

There was plenty of work to be had in 1960s Yorkshire; Brendan turned his hand to labouring on the M1 motorway, and then decided to box. Although his own career, which ended at the age of 33, was not a world-beating one, it taught Brendan the sport – or art – from the bottom up. His experience of lower division scraps in Europe and the UK, from gyms to working men's clubs where he notched up a few wins but mostly just bruises, taught him not only how to fight, but also how to train for the bout. It didn't take a genius to tell Ingle that, unlike his brother Johnny (a European champ), he was never going to be a serious contender for a national, let alone world title, but the man's natural intelligence did tell him that he could help others.

To this end he had also taken over training at the local Wincobank youth club, a club that he was to bless with international fame in the ensuing years. When his fighting career ground to an ageing halt, he turned his attention full-time to nurturing the talent that he saw around him.

What he also saw was a stagnation in training methods and boxing in his adoptive town. So, with the support of his wife Alma, Brendan set out to train new methods into his boys. Not content with the straightforward orthodox approach – right-handed fighters predominated so right-handed boxing was the norm – he also actively taught 'southpaw' or left-handed. This was to pay dividends when he encountered the seven-year old, ambidextrous Naseem Hamed years later. But for now it enabled his young charges to see and experience every aspect of the ring-art. Footwork, sparring, fitness and the intelligence needed to survive in the ring were all taught at Brendan's gym, which went from strength to strength.

But life was not to continue as smoothly as Brendan and Alma had planned. Despite training national champions and creating an ethos which lifted not only the club but the city itself from depression to recognition, the Amateur Boxing Association decided to clamp down. A new ruling made it clear that pros and amateurs couldn't be trained in the same gym. Making the decision for the Ingles, the ABA kicked the club out, forcing it to concentrate on pro boxing – which, of course, they excelled at.

The most famous name to emerge from Ingle's patronage prior to the Prince was Herol 'Bomber' Graham, who was to become one of Naz's early heroes. Brendan not only trained but

A savvy mentor: at the dingy church hall which is St. Thomas's Boys' Club in Sheffield's Wincobank area, Brendan Ingle has produced champions like Herol 'Bomber' Graham, Johnny Nelson and the

also 'named' the quiet 'Bomber' to the British and European light-middleweight and middleweight titles through the 1980s. And it's this naming – some might say 'hyping' – of his fighters that is another hallmark of the savvy Irishman.

Having achieved massive continental success with Graham, Brendan was left with a single, stirring and motivating dream. To train a world champion. And when Naz's father brought the seven-year-old through the doors of St. Thomas's, canny Brendan felt somewhere that the cocky youngster could well be the answer to that dream.

Prince Naseem Hamed. Brendan trains amateurs, professionals, blacks and whites, champions and delinquents. His motto: 'Only you are responsible for yourself.'

ABOVE BY ANTON WANT; RIGHT BY JOHN GICHIGI: ALLSPORT
PAGES 12–13 BY BEN RADFORD (LEFT); MARK THOMPSON (RIGHT): ALLSPORT

1992-1997

RICKY BEARD

FIGHT 1
14 APRIL 1992
MANSFIELD LEISURE CENTRE

Ricky Beard:
"I thought he was just a flashy kid and I could go out, meet him head on and knock him out"

Result: Naz wins with a Second-Round-right to the solar plexus; KO at 2 minutes, 36 seconds!

Round 1
The Prince begins as a southpaw but has to duck out of the way of Beard's attacking bombs – Beard lands two right-crosses. Naz goes up a gear, and into the second half of the round he decks Beard with a two-handed combination to his chin. Beard stays down for a count of two.

Round 2
The bell sounds and Naz bloodies Beard's nose with a scorching punch. Beard's guard stays up, and the Prince has to punch through it. He uses his speed and agility and manages to time a right-hand to the solar plexus. Beard stays down for the count, and it's all over.

Fight Statistics

REFEREE	Mr Thomas
OPPONENT	Ricky Beard
NATIONALITY	English
AGE	29
HEIGHT	5ft 8in, 1.73m
WEIGHT	8st 2lb, 51.7kg
NAZ'S WEIGHT	8st 2lb, 51.7kg
RECORD	W2–L6–D1
HONOURS	Former NE London ABA Champion
RANKED	British No 6 (Flyweight)
NAZ'S PREDICTION	None this time

Ready for my close-up, Mr. De Mille?: Naz has always known the value of showmanship – and that starts with making a good entrance.

'Come on, get me!' Many boxers will learn to their cost in the years ahead that Naz is most dangerous when he lets them inside his guard, as Tom Johnson does in the 1997 bout, but to no avail – down he goes in Round Eight.

John Morris, General Secretary of the British Board of Boxing Control doesn't like the Prince's antics: "Cut it out!"

SHAUN NORMAN

FIGHT 2
25 APRIL 1992
MANCHESTER

Fight Statistics

REFEREE	Roy Snipe
OPPONENT	Shaun Norman
NATIONALITY	English
AGE	22
HEIGHT	5ft 4in
WEIGHT	8st 12lb 8oz, 56.5kg
NAZ'S WEIGHT	8st 2lb, 51.7kg
RECORD	W1–L3–D0
HONOURS	Finalist in the Midlands ABA Flyweight
RANKED	Not ranked
NAZ'S PREDICTION	None this time

Result: Naz wins with a right in the Second Round!

Round 1
Norman, despite his lack of ranking, is no easy touch and is expected to offer more competition than Beard, according to the people 'who know'. Naz, of course, doesn't realise this and takes a few punches in the early part of the round. Waking up to his task, he puts Norman down for a count of three with a left-cross. Norman is bleeding as he returns to his corner.

Round 2
Naz is in his element as he show-boats around both boxer and ring, seemingly uncaring for any punches that might, but don't land. The entertaining over, he lands a right on Norman, who goes down and doesn't look like coming back up. The ref counts '8' and ends the fight with 2 minutes and 5 seconds remaining. The bout does plenty for Naz's growing reputation, earning him plaudits from the boxing press. The establishment still doesn't like his style, however...

FIGHT 3
23 MAY 1992
BIRMINGHAM

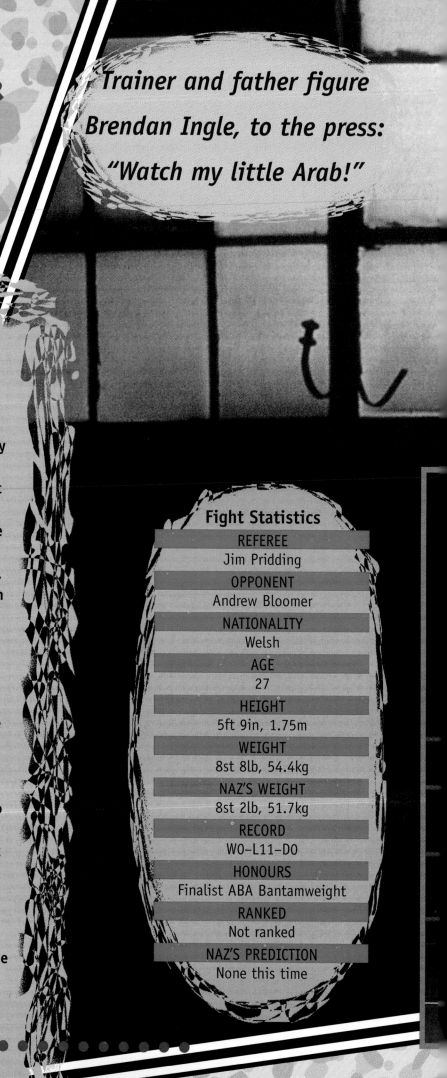

Trainer and father figure Brendan Ingle, to the press: "Watch my little Arab!"

Result: Naz right-hooks Bloomer in Round 2 as the Ref steps in

Round 1

Bloomer is not the man his 11-loss record would have you believe. Knocked down only once, his losses have come on points or TKOs. He's a stayer, a scrapper; he's a great deal taller and a great deal more experienced than his opponent. But no one seems to have told this to Naseem Hamed, who proceeds to land hooks, right and left, and uppercuts, ensuring that the Welshman returns to his worried seconds with blood streaming from his nose.

Round 2

Bloomer emerges from towel and bucket with intent – he swings and misses. Maybe this wakes Naz to the realisation that the Second has been his lucky round so far. He cannons the Welshman with stunning combinations, pinning him to the ropes, so he is unable to escape and can't retaliate. Either bored, or sensing the quick kill, Naz uses that devastating right-hook again to fell Bloomer. All this and there's still 2 minutes and 14 seconds remaining in the round. Referee Pridding doesn't see it continuing, however, and puts an end to the bout. Naz has yet to finish two rounds in his Pro career. Bloomer is destroyed. Naz somersaults!

Fight Statistics

REFEREE	Jim Pridding
OPPONENT	Andrew Bloomer
NATIONALITY	Welsh
AGE	27
HEIGHT	5ft 9in, 1.75m
WEIGHT	8st 8lb, 54.4kg
NAZ'S WEIGHT	8st 2lb, 51.7kg
RECORD	W0–L11–D0
HONOURS	Finalist ABA Bantamweight
RANKED	Not ranked
NAZ'S PREDICTION	None this time

Left: Brendan's 'little Arab' has little time for Welsh pretenders to his throne, as he takes a moment out from dispatching Andrew Bloomer.

MAIN BY AL BELLO; INSET BY JOHN GICHIGI: ALLSPORT

NICHOLAS MATTHEWS

FIGHT 4
14 JULY 1992
GROSVENOR HOUSE HOTEL, LONDON

Result: Oh boy, Naz doesn't do it in two! Round 3, the Ref steps in.

Round 1
This is a special fight for Naz. Not only is it his first in London as a Pro, it's also being staged at the benefit for the popular Michael Watson, who'd nearly died a year earlier after taking punishment from that other 'entertainer', Chris Eubank. The whole British boxing world attends the occasion. Naz doesn't see it as make-or-break, he sees it as a golden chance to really show the people who matter just what he's capable of. Because of the flak he received after the Bloomer fight, maybe the Prince is actually trying to find out about the other fighter. Whatever the reason, Naz circles and probes Matthews rather than unleashing any of his growing arsenal of punches, combinations, hooks and uppercuts.

Round 2
The probing, the good behaviour – the complete un-Nazmanship, is over as both boxers emerge from the security of the seconds into the battlefield. In the face of promoters, TV and news journalists, administrators and fans, Naz puts Matthews down with a right to the head. Unaware that he's in with one of history's Greats, the Welshman gets up after a five-count from referee Francis. The bell sounds with the Prince ready for 'the kill'. Both men make their way to safety.

'Miguel' takes Naz
to three.

JOHN GICHIGI: ALLSPORT

Fight Statistics

REFEREE
Roy Francis

OPPONENT
Nicholas 'Miguel' Matthews

NATIONALITY
Welsh

AGE
26

HEIGHT
5ft 7in, 1.70m

WEIGHT
8st 10lb, 55.3kg

NAZ'S WEIGHT
8st 7lb 5oz, 54.1kg

RECORD
W6–L37–D8

HONOURS
None

RANKED
Not ranked

NAZ'S PREDICTION
None this time

Round 3

This is uncharted territory for the Sheffield lad, but he's the one making the maps as he destroys 'Miguel' in a series of terrifyingly fast and accurate onslaughts. The action is too much for the referee on this night of nights, and with 1 minute and 55 seconds remaining of the three-minute round, he's forced to put an end to Naz's fun and Matthew's humiliation. The fight is won. The style is electric. Naz has arrived in the 'Smoke'. But his night isn't over yet. The boxing establishment, awed if still annoyed, award 'The Outstanding Prospect of the Year' trophy to the Prince on this same evening.

DES GARGANO

FIGHT 5
7 OCTOBER 1992
SUNDERLAND

Result: Are we getting old? Four rounds to take out the Manchester man!

Round 1
The Prince has known Gargano for some years, they've sparred and they like each other. But that, of course, is outside the ring. This bout will show everybody that Brendan's 'little Arab' was nowhere to be seen when the compassion genes were handed out. Unlike the Matthews fight, there's no holding back as Gargano goes down for the count of '6!', and then down again, only to be saved by the sanctuary sound of the bell. Naz has foxed him as well as punched him, dancing around his old friend with breathtaking speed. As he returns to his seconds, the Mancunian knows he's facing his toughest battle yet.

Round 2
Naseem Hamed wants this over fast. Although staying for a few rounds might entertain the crowd, the Prince doesn't enjoy the humiliation he's dishing out. Down goes Gargano once again, felled by an airborne assault, as his nemesis dances around him. But Des wants to make a fight of it and is up fast, trying to return fire, looking for weakness where there is none. The bell sounds with no hope for one, and no mercy from the other.

Des Gargano, magnanimous in defeat: "Naseem is really classy"

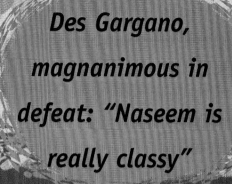

Round 3
This is becoming a long-haul. Gargano offers more opposition than the youngster had planned for. Could it be that there's some doubt in the Prince's mind over converting his pal from man to mash? No way. Naseem Hamed sweeps any doubts, any problems from his mind as he feints and shimmies around the ring, around HIS ring. Almost inevitably, the Lancastrian bites the canvas for a third time. But again there's no count. Again he rises and returns to the fray for more punishment. And still Naz can't finish him.

Round 4
Too long. Too many minutes. Too much of a fight, as Gargano seems steadfast in his refusal to capitulate. But brave as he may be, Des is offering nothing in response to Naz's jinks, jabs and combinations. Eventually cornered, he receives an agonising left-hand to his chest and, unable to breathe, his body refuses to respond any longer. Referee Watson, with 54 seconds left on his watch, is forced to put an end to the savage out-classing.

David and Goliath: while struggling to find worthy opponents in 1992, little could Naz have realised that one day Frank Bruno would crown him Prince.

JOHN GICHIGI: ALLSPORT

Fight Statistics

REFEREE	Gerry Watson
OPPONENT	Des Gargano
NATIONALITY	Welsh
AGE	26
HEIGHT	5ft 5in, 1.65m
WEIGHT	8st 10lb, 55.3kg
NAZ'S WEIGHT	8st 9lb, 54.9kg
RECORD	W26–L58–D2
HONOURS	None
RANKED	Not ranked
NAZ'S PREDICTION	None this time

FIGHT 6
12 NOVEMBER 1992
EVERTON SPORTS CENTRE, LIVERPOOL

An audience with the crowned Prince: As Naseem's renown grows, it isn't only the ring entrances that become grander, so do the post-fight press conferences. This one below is after the 1996 Alicea fight in Newcastle.

Result: Too many fights in 1992, or better opposition. Points decide it after 6.

Rounds 1–3

The Prince, always super-fit, despite his love of chocolate, is giving three pounds to the taller man... like that should matter! But maybe the Gargano fight just 38 days before, together with the five other bouts already this year, have taken their toll. The first round points the way for the rest of the bout, as Buckley shuts up shop, forcing Naz to explore as well as entertain. In Round Two the Prince is at once annoyed and frustrated by the tactics of his non-opponent. Buckley raises his guard as if it was a ten-foot thick portcullis, forcing the champion-in-waiting to grapple rather than dance. If this keeps up we could be looking at a points decision for the first time – and this just does not fit the game-plan. Naz invites the Brummie to punch him – no reply. The bell sounds. And it's more of the same in the third, and this time a warning to Naseem – hitting and holding is not in the rules; but the rules don't legislate for the stonewalling that Naz is being forced to contend with. So Naz descends to his foe's level. He chats and goads, he

Naz on the money he needs: *"One billion pounds should just about do it"*

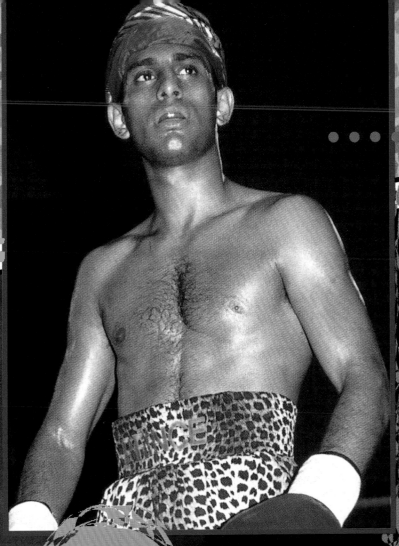

Photo credit: JOHN GICHIGI: ALLSPORT

Fight Statistics

REFEREE	Phil Cowswill
OPPONENT	Peter Buckley
NATIONALITY	English
AGE	23
HEIGHT	5ft 8in, 1.73m
WEIGHT	8st 10lb 8oz, 55.6kg
NAZ'S WEIGHT	8st 7lb 8oz, 54.2kg
RECORD	W18–L18–D5
HONOURS	Midlands Super-Featherweight Champion
RANKED	Not ranked
NAZ'S PREDICTION	None this time

holds, and yet from somewhere comes a points-worthy punch that introduces Buckley to the canvas. But it's only for a '2' count, and the dirge begins again.

Rounds 4–6
Bring down the wall! The Prince's mind and spirit are attuned to elegance and supersonic speed. Brendan has trained him this way. He uses orthodox and southpaw, he digs into his reserves for the knowledge bestowed on him at St. Thomas's. But it's still to no avail, as his opponent's professional self-protection continues to deny the final punch. In the fifth, Naz knows what he's got to do – he invites Buckley by dropping his own guard time and again, to the astonishment of the audience. In order to make the most of these invitations, Buckley, like a Klingon battle-cruiser dropping its cloak before firing, must drop his guard. Yet the only thing to drop is the bell-man's hand on the lever as the round ends in frustration again. As Round Six starts, it's clear the fight has gone the distance. Brendan is confident, he's seen it all before and knows that this is the kind of education that Naseem needs and that the Prince will benefit from this dreadful drudgery. Next time will be different. But now, despite staggering Buckley with a left just before the bell, it's going to be a points decision. Thankfully for boxing, negativity doesn't win fights, and Naz is victorious by four rounds to the Midlander's one. It's time to go home and take in the lessons learnt.

Above: Naz swaps crown for turban to meet Picardi in 1994.

MAIN BY MARK THOMPSON: ALLSPORT

1993

Prince Naseem Hamed: *"In my eyes nothing can stop me from being a legend"*

Fight Statistics

REFEREE	Roy Francis
OPPONENT	Alan Ley
NATIONALITY	Welsh
AGE	24
HEIGHT	5ft 8in, 1.73m
WEIGHT	8st 6lb, 53.5kg
NAZ'S WEIGHT	8st 5lb 8oz, 53.3kg
RECORD	W4–L0–D0
HONOURS	Welsh ABA Flyweight Champion
RANKED	Not ranked
NAZ'S PREDICTION	None this time

Naz has a thing about cars, but this New York limo may be stretching the point a bit far.

Result: Back to winning ways as Naz takes him down in Round 2. KO!

Round 1

Not quite making the 8st 6lb weight for the fight, and wanting to shake off the bad press he'd attracted from the Buckley bout, Naz comes out with all guns blazing. Ley is no pussy, but seems to want to find a quiet place to lick his wounds as the Prince creams him with punch after punch. Usually a left-hander will cause problems to an orthodox boxer, but Ley's southpaw nature is no problem for the ambidextrous Naseem. St. Thomas's lessons, now second nature, enable the Sheffield teenager to batter his older opponent from every angle. One set of punches levels Ley, who only just makes it up with one count of the nine remaining.

Round 2

Returning to the squared circle, the former Welsh champ hangs on, literally, for all he's worth. Buoyed up by his first-round knockdown, Naz proceeds to teach some of his own lessons, show-boating maybe a little less, he takes his foe down once, and then does it again with a series of undefendable shots to head and body. Enough is looking like more than plenty as Ley feels the canvas meet his body for a fourth and final time tonight. Despite being aware of what is going on around him, he is in no condition to do anything about it and the bout goes to Naz in a show of sheer brilliance.

Prince Naseem Hamed:
"I'm good enough to win the British title right now"

FIGHT 8
26 MAY 1993
MANSFIELD LEISURE CENTRE

Result: The referee has to stop the assault in Round 3. Naz wins again!

Round 1
Kevin Jenkins is not the kind of opponent Naz should be facing at this stage in his career. A pleasant enough chap, the Welshman has little to offer in terms of competition or lessons to be learnt. This is almost a spar for Naz, who begins as he means to go on, gobsmacking the crowd with his shenanigans, dancing, feinting, dropping his guard, all the old tricks. Jenkins has more than his gob smacked, however, as his entire body – well, those elements that are legal to hit – are showered with a vicious storm of blows. This is Naz at play, the next round will up the tempo.

Round 2
Slam! Another shot sweeps through what is left of Jenkins' defences. The dancing and prancing is minimised as the onslaught reaches new levels of harshness. Although Jenkins attempts to return fire using the all that he can muster, he's trapped in a corner and almost demolished by the blitzkrieg speed of Naz's assault. This can't go on much longer and the bell can't ring too soon. But it does.

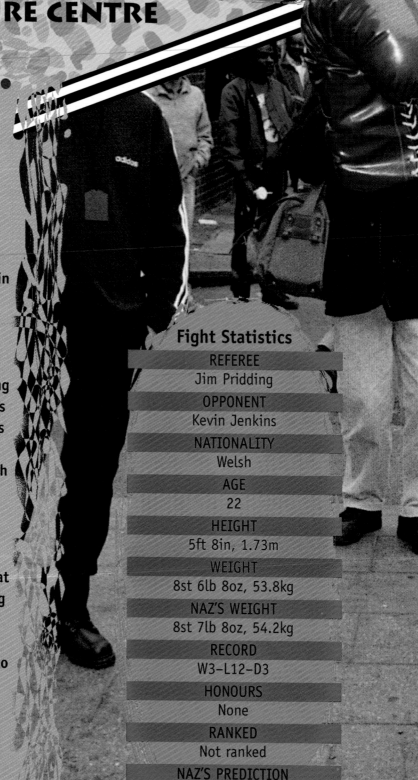

Fight Statistics

REFEREE	Jim Pridding
OPPONENT	Kevin Jenkins
NATIONALITY	Welsh
AGE	22
HEIGHT	5ft 8in, 1.73m
WEIGHT	8st 6lb 8oz, 53.8kg
NAZ'S WEIGHT	8st 7lb 8oz, 54.2kg
RECORD	W3–L12–D3
HONOURS	None
RANKED	Not ranked
NAZ'S PREDICTION	None this time

Round 3
Referee Jim Pridding, with all his experience, is keeping a weather-eye on this uneven match; he's aware that something has to give and he doesn't want any tragedy to mar his, or the fighters', records. The Prince pounds, he reigns in the ring and rains down the fire from his lightning-fast fists. That's it, with 1 minute and 2 seconds left in the round, Kevin Jenkins is trapped beneath an avalanche of blows. Jim Pridding calls a halt to the carnage and Prince Naseem Hamed is victorious once again. After the fight, however, the laid-back Jenkins disputes the nature of the victory, declaring that he's been hit harder before. Maybe his memory has been affected?

My, what big fists you have, granny: Rapper Normski sets out to rearrange Naseem's pretty face.

STU FORSTER: ALLSPORT

CHRIS CLARKSON

FIGHT 9
24 SEPTEMBER 1993
NATIONAL BASKETBALL ARENA, DUBLIN, IRELAND

Fashion accessories: Naz diplays his superior colour co-ordination in mouthwear below – training is a less glamorous affair.

Result: It's that golden round again. Round 2. KO!

Round 1

It has been a good year for Naz, with recognition for his skill and derision for his style coming in equal measure. Clarkson is no easy touch for the last fight of the year. Naz appears less showmanlike and more workmanlike in this first round, as if he wants to show the Irish crowd his boxing skills rather than the razzmatazz. In no uncertain terms he forces Clarkson to the floor with a left late in the round, but the Hull-born 'Yorkshireman' makes it through just about intact.

Round 2

It's a well known fact that Naz doesn't touch booze of any kind, his religion doesn't permit it, his training won't allow it, but maybe he wants to get the bout over with and visit the Guinness brewery, because he starts punching hard and extremely fast, rarely missing. Down goes Clarkson to a right-cross. Up he gets again, but visibly weakened. Then, with 1 minute and 10 seconds left, and the fight it now proves to be, referee Wilson looks down on the once more floored fighter and says the word all boxers fear most: 'Ten!'. Clarkson is out, demolished and barely aware of what is going on around him. It's a victorious return home for Brendan Ingle, and a suitable way to finish the boxing year for the still-teen Naseem.

Fight Statistics

REFEREE	**NAZ'S WEIGHT**
Barney Wilson	8st 10lb, 55.3kg
OPPONENT	**RECORD**
Chris Clarkson	W18–L21–D2
NATIONALITY	**HONOURS**
English	IBF Intercontinental
AGE	Bantamweight
26	Challenger
HEIGHT	**RANKED**
5ft 4in, 1.63m	Not ranked
WEIGHT	**NAZ'S PREDICTION**
8st 12lb, 56.2kg	None this time

ABOVE BY JOHN GICHIGI; RIGHT BY AL BELLO: ALLSPORT

TRULY
'PRINCE' NASEEM,
SETTING HIS SIGHTS ON CHALLENGING
FOR THE CHAMPIONSHIPS, POSES FOR THE
CAMERAS DRESSED AS A YEMENI (PRINCE?)

Naz, pictured in May 1996, reflects on the material things in life his boxing success is bringing him

STU FORSTER: ALLSPORT

FIGHT 10   PETER BUCKLEY
24 FEBRUARY 1994
CARDIFF ICE RINK

Fight Statistics

REFEREE	Roy Francis
OPPONENT	Peter Buckley
NATIONALITY	English
AGE	25
HEIGHT	5ft 8in, 1.73m
WEIGHT	8st 10lb, 55.3kg
NAZ'S WEIGHT	8st 10lb, 55.3kg
RECORD	W18–L29–D5
HONOURS	Midlands Super-Featherweight Champion; WBO Pentacontinental Super-Bantamweight Challenger
RANKED	Not ranked
NAZ'S PREDICTION	None this time

Result: Buckley again, this time it's in four as Naz wipes the floor, or does he?

Round 1
When these two last met the fighting was scrapping and the result came on points. This time around a more mature Naseem comes at his task with greater professionalism. Okay, so he jinxes and feints – there's no way he can help that, it's his way – but, like the town of his upbringing in its heyday, there's more steel in Naz than simple glitter. This is a boxer whom he wants to box... hard.

Rounds 2–3
As before, Buckley retreats behind his well-worn protective guard. But he's savvy enough to realise that counter-attacking might be his only hope. This time Naz is more relaxed, he doesn't get called by the ref, he fights his fight. Occasionally he offers himself up to attack, but the bait is far too colourful for his opponent. In the third round Buckley manages to land a glancing blow, but this is still Naz's fight. Still Buckley retreats and boxes on from his now-familiar guard. The Prince, instead of taking Buckley at his own game, simply piles in punch after punch and offers himself up again and again... but still no joy.

Round 4
Naz unleashes some jarring blows, taking little or nothing in reprisal for his actions and, with 1 minute 12 seconds left, the fight is stopped. Informed sources say that the referee halted this fight too early, that it would have gone the full six, but the referee must have realised that at 4–0 down, there was nothing left for Buckley to fight on for, except maybe serious injury. So chalk up another win for Naseem Hamed.

Prince Naseem Hamed:
"Oh baby, it hurts to be this good"

FIGHT 11
12 APRIL 1994
MANSFIELD LEISURE CENTRE

Prince Naseem Hamed:
"When they write these stupid things in Boxing News and the rest, I just laugh"

Result: One round is all that's needed to beat the Belgian. KO!

Round 1

Miceli has some form, more wins than losses, he's under 30, and he has a national title to his name. Unlike Buckley in the previous bout, he's also an attacking fighter. So when he rises from the deck, having been drilled with a Naseem right-hander shortly after the fight begins, he goes on the offensive. Maybe Buckley could have given him some sound advice on how to go the distance with the Prince, because all-out attack is simply not good enough to do the job. Before he knows what or who has hit him, he's tasting floor once again. Again he rises, fighting for pride rather than any sense of reality against the deluge of punches that nearly wash him from the town, let alone the ring. Naz is cooking on propane now: right, right, blow after blow shatters the Belgian until he's finally floored with a left that targets his head like a SCUD. The chances are that Miceli can't even hear the referee reaching the '10!' count – all he's aware of is the taste of defeat and the thump of Naz's victory dance. Another one well and truly gnaws at the dust.

Fight Statistics

REFEREE	John Coyle
OPPONENT	John Miceli
NATIONALITY	Belgian
AGE	26
HEIGHT	5ft 8in, 1,73m
WEIGHT	8st 8lb 8oz, 54.7kg
NAZ'S WEIGHT	8st 10lb, 55.3kg
RECORD	W10–L02–01
HONOURS	Belgian Featherweight Champion
RANKED	Not ranked
NAZ'S PREDICTION	'He'll fall in six'

Mark Thompson: Allsport

VINCENZO BELCASTRO

FIGHT 12
11 MAY 1994
PONDS FORGE ARENA, SHEFFIELD
EUROPEAN BANTAMWEIGHT TITLE CHALLENGE

Result: The toughest of them all? Naz is taken to 12 rounds before winning!

Miceli receives the Princely ring-entry treatment – but it's only a quick visit for Naz, unlike his next fight.

Round 1

How much pressure does one man need to survive? It is as if Naz's management want their boy – no longer a teen – to sweat it with more riding on one fight than most men could handle.

Right! It's his first major home town bout!

Left! It's a European title fight, and Naz hasn't even won a British title yet!

Smash! It's against a fighter at the peak of his form, with a possible American bout as the prize!

Belcastro, at 33, has been most places and boxed most styles. He's no mug and has a record to prove it. Not only this, but Naz is also fighting up a weight on his normal featherweight. Wearing his now trademark leopard skin trunks, the Prince storms out of his corner. Fighting the only way he knows how, he floors the stunned Italian within the first minute of the

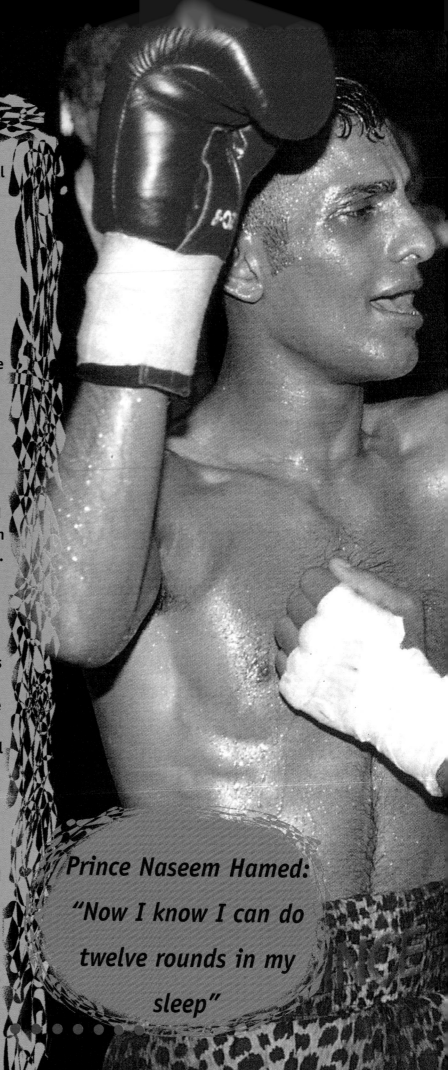

round. The way to win this bout is to take control, and once he's got it, keep it with all the power that comes with God-given talent and Ingle-trained skill.

Rounds 2–4

Belcastro is dumbed by the torrent of punches coming at him from nowhere and everywhere. He seems unable to track the smaller man, let alone hang a meaningful punch on him. So, like a good pro should, he trusts to stamina and ring-savvy. He knows that Hamed has never gone more than six rounds since turning professional in 1992. He also knows that he himself has fought the distance against bigger, more experienced fighters in his long and distinguished career. Reeling from the speed if nothing else, he settles in for the duration – a standing Champ always has to be beaten.

Rounds 5–7

If Belcastro can go the distance, he can still hope to salvage the bout on points. He does his best to retain dignity and guard, but he's never come close to anybody as quick as the Prince. Naz, with experience gained from the Buckley brawls, still seems to be in a world of his own. Like a batsman who sees the ball not at hand- but at basketball-size, he seems incapable of missing. Again and again punches land on the body, the head, the face. Belcastro tries the street-fighting approach, tight, occasionally on the sly side of the laws. Maybe he can intimidate the lad into capitulation.

Rounds 8–10

Both fighters flirt with lawlessness as they embrace in unholy hugs. Elbows fly, digs and nudges seek out weaknesses. No one thinks

JOHN GICHIGI: ALLSPORT

Prince Naseem Hamed: *"Now I know I can do twelve rounds in my sleep"*

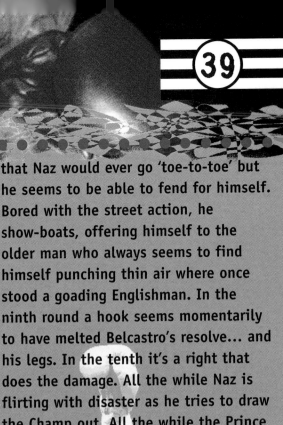

that Naz would ever go 'toe-to-toe' but he seems to be able to fend for himself. Bored with the street action, he show-boats, offering himself to the older man who always seems to find himself punching thin air where once stood a goading Englishman. In the ninth round a hook seems momentarily to have melted Belcastro's resolve... and his legs. In the tenth it's a right that does the damage. All the while Naz is flirting with disaster as he tries to draw the Champ out. All the while the Prince looks more like a king!

Rounds 11–12

Belcastro hits the floor in Round 11. The people who said that Naseem Hamed was too young, too inexperienced, had only fought ring fodder and would be taught a lesson by the Italian, are starting to heat up their humble pies (and stir the gravy in their numerous hats) ready for a feast of apology. But Belcastro rises. The auditorium is transifxed as the two men go at it again and again. Has Naz done enough to take the title on points? Can he take his man down and win with glory? Hamed and his corner know the answer as he goes in for the final round. History will re-tell over and over the astonishing last round of this fight, in which Naseem Hamed wins without even trying to land a meaningful punch. Instead he dances. He grimaces and smiles, not at his opponent but at the crowd and the cameras. He's like a hero returning from a conquest rather than one in the midst of the battle. The round ends and Naz has tamed his man. He is a Champion.

Fight Statistics

REFEREE	Bob Logist
OPPONENT	Vincenzo Belcastro
NATIONALITY	Italian
AGE	33
HEIGHT	5ft 8in, 1.73m
WEIGHT	8st 4lb 12oz, 52.9kg
NAZ'S WEIGHT	8st 6lb, 53.5kg
RECORD	W28–L06–03
HONOURS	European Bantamweight Champion
RANKED	World Number 6 (WBC)
NAZ'S PREDICTION	None this time

*Prince Naseem Hamed:
"I will not change my style for anybody"*

FIGHT 13
17 AUGUST 1994
HILLSBOROUGH LEISURE CENTRE, SHEFFIELD
EUROPEAN BANTAMWEIGHT TITLE CHALLENGE
– FIRST DEFENCE

Result: No more 12 rounders! Call the Ref in Round 3!

Round 1
Another Italian, another bout on home turf. Picardi has beaten Belcastro, but that was nearly ten years ago. Some people have been saying that Picardi is merely here for the ride, he's well past his not-so-impressive prime. But they always seem to say that about Naz's opponents. Naz doesn't mind, and springs around the ring punching and prancing. He takes Picardi down with a combination, but the Italian rises again, only to walk into a Naz left-hander. The round is the Prince's.

Round 2
Left, left, left and more lefts. Picardi goes down but the referee calls it a slip, and maybe even a push from the Sheffield wonder. Never mind, the Italian goes down once again, and this time for a count. He's up in time and far from happy with the count decision. The anger does him good as he manages to land a punch on Naseem. The left-hook looks bad but Naz seems unbothered by it. Round Two to the Prince.

Fight Statistics

REFEREE
Knud Jensen

OPPONENT
Antonio Picardi

NATIONALITY
Italian

AGE
31

HEIGHT
5ft 8in, 1.73m

WEIGHT
8st 5lb, 53.1kg

NAZ'S WEIGHT
8st 5lb 12oz, 53.4kg

RECORD
W24–L10–D0

HONOURS
Italian Bantamweight Champion

RANKED
World Number 25 (WBC):
European Number 1 (EBU)

NAZ'S PREDICTION
'Three rounds, that's
my prediction.'

Round 3
Picardi goes down twice, once from a fall, the next time from a fair punch. He rises on '4!' and walks straight back into nine punches in combination and at blinding speed. There's no way he can survive this, and with 1 minute 74 seconds remaining in the round, the referee counts him out. Maybe the former Italian Champ was just along for the ride... only it didn't look that way. Whatever the pre-fight thinking, post-fight he's destroyed.

BOTH BY JOHN GICHIGI: ALLSPORT

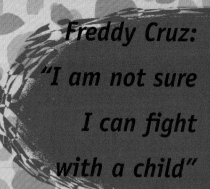

Freddy Cruz:
"I am not sure
I can fight
with a child"

FIGHT 14
12 OCTOBER 1994

PONDS FORGE ARENA, SHEFFIELD
VACANT WBC INTERNATIONAL
SUPER-BANTAMWEIGHT CHAMPIONSHIP

Fight Statistics

REFEREE	Larry O'Connell
OPPONENT	Freddy Cruz
NATIONALITY	Dominican
AGE	32
HEIGHT	5ft 8in, 1.73m
WEIGHT	8st 9lb, 54.9kg
NAZ'S WEIGHT	8st 9lb 8oz, 55kg
RECORD	W44–L6–D6
HONOURS	None
RANKED	Not ranked
NAZ'S PREDICTION	None at this time

Result: Call the referee to stop this in Round 6!

Rounds 1–3

Cruz is a proposition. Despite not holding a belt, he has also never been put down, and is renowned for an excellent defence. His ability to punch is also not disputed. All this is good pro stuff, but Naz doesn't box like a good pro, and this confuses the Dominican. Both men land hard punches in the first round, and Cruz appears to change his initial impression of 'the child'. The next two rounds are torrid, to say the least, with Cruz complaining of low blows, and both fighters trading punches, if not in speed and accuracy, then at least with the same venom.

Rounds 4–6

A right from Naz, a left from Cruz. Then both men go down in a pile caused by their own momentum. Cruz rises only to see Naz doing a back-flip, landing in a fight-ready stance, and smiling at both opponent and assembled media. The fifth sees Cruz warned for hitting while holding, a sure sign that the fighter is tiring in the face of the Sheffield Champ's

'Who are you calling a kid?' Unfortunately for Freddy Cruz, this 'child' proves to be a bit more than a mere strutting bantam…

onslaught. Naz, as usual, still seems to be as fit as he was when he flipped over the ropes and into the ring. Then, in the sixth, Naz throws what has since become a legendary punch. He looks as if he's going for a blow to the body but changes direction in mid-throw to crunch into Cruz's face. Despite its brilliance, this still isn't the knock-out blow – this comes seconds later in the form of an upper-cut that forces the referee to intervene and call off the fight. Cruz, who has never been put down, is beaten. Naz wins yet another belt.

Prince Naseem Hamed: "I don't go out with the intention of getting anyone put in hospital. I just want to win"

FREDDY CRUZ DEALT WITH, AND NASEEM HOLDER OF THE PREVIOUSLY VACANT WBC INTERNATIONAL SUPER-BANTAMWEIGHT CHAMPIONSHIP, HE NOW FACES A CHALLENGE FROM LAUREANO RAMIREZ, WHO RECKONS HE CAN TAKE IT OFF THE PRINCE.

JOHN GICHIGI: ALLSPORT

FIGHT 15, 19 NOVEMBER 1994

CARDIFF ICE RINK

LAUREANO RAMIREZ

DEFENCE OF WBC INT.

SUPER-BANTAMWEIGHT CHAMPIONSHIP

Result: Round 3, and it's time to pack your bags!

Rounds 1–2

Naz has never been popular in Wales, maybe that's why he keeps fighting there... the abuse he receives from the crowd gees him up. And he needs some motivation because the flu has been the nearest foe to deck him since he began boxing. Recovering from the illness has taken its toll, and the first two rounds are nothing to write home about. Ramirez shows himself to be quick and able to defend himself, although few, if any, punches find their way to an off-colour Prince. As the fight wears on you can see Naz trying to build to some kind of finale, but it's a struggle.

They always start standing up but so often seem to end up lying down...

Fight Statistics

REFEREE	NAZ'S WEIGHT
Mickey Vann	8st 10lb, 55.3kg
OPPONENT	RECORD
Laureano 'Padilla' Ramirez	W17–L0–D1
NATIONALITY	HONOURS
Dominican	IBF Intercontinental Bantamweight Champion
AGE	
28	
HEIGHT	RANKED
5ft 8in, 1.73m	World Number 3 (IBF)
WEIGHT	NAZ'S PREDICTION
8st 8lb 10oz, 54.7kg	None this time

Round 3

Both men decide to go up a level and actually land some punches that make sense of the bout (and nonsense of the human body). There's nothing like 15 minutes in an incredibly humid atmosphere, dancing around a ring, to sweat out the flu, especially if you're usually as fit as Naz. There's some holding, which annoys the free-flowing Naseem, who throws Ramirez canvasward before battering him, so that the ref is forced to step in. Seconds later, Ramirez is back for more, a dumb move considering that Naz has had enough. Slamming in a right to the jaw, the Prince puts his foe to the deck one more time, and this time Referee Vann stops the fight as a no-hoper for the challenger. Another Welsh victory for Naz.

Prince Naseem Hamed: "I am another legend coming through"

BOTH BY JOHN GICHIGI: ALLSPORT

GOODBYE 1994. NAZ IS THE EUROPEAN BANTAMWEIGHT AND WBC INTERNATIONAL SUPER-BANTAMWEIGHT CHAMP. HE HOPES 1995 WILL BRING PLENTY MORE CHALLENGERS TO HIS SUPREMACY.

1995

ARMANDO CASTRO

FIGHT 16
21 JANUARY 1995
SCOTTISH CONFERENCE CENTRE, GLASGOW
DEFENCE OF WBC INT. SUPER-BANTAMWEIGHT CHAMPIONSHIP

Fight Statistics

REFEREE	Mickey Vann
OPPONENT	Armando Castro
NATIONALITY	Mexican
AGE	31
HEIGHT	5ft 5in, 1.65m
WEIGHT	8st 10lb, 55.3kg
NAZ'S WEIGHT	8st 9lb 12oz, 55.2kg
RECORD	W42–L17–D03
HONOURS	Mexican Featherweight Champion
RANKED	Not Ranked
NAZ'S PREDICTION	'He will not go beyond five.'

Result: The Mexican hits the floor in 4. Win to Naz!

Rounds 1–2

Castro isn't much like real competition, it has to be said. He's never achieved much and is largely Naz fodder, fight food to keep the Prince match-fit until he can get a shot at the big fish. So Naz snarls out of his corner with all guns blazing. He doesn't bother to show off much at first, being happy to land some good old left-hands on the already astonished Mexican. Unlike the Welsh crowd, the Scots love the Prince, and love his antics. But all doesn't go to plan, as the Mexican manages to put a fist-filled left glove hooking into the Prince. And there is more: Castro actually adopts the Naz role of signalling his opponent to come and get him! He's warned for this, but you can see that the Mexican is up for it, despite his lack of speed. Round Two, and Naz places Castro on the deck with a left, however the referee sees it as a slip and the fight goes on. Down goes the challenger again, and Naz is developing the look of a man who can't spell 'mercy', let alone offer it.

Rounds 3–4

At last a fighter who really wants to hit the small Sheffield stallion. Castro emerges from his corner looking battered but prepared to punch. Naz is in little danger as he dances around the onslaught, but Castro is winning the crowd over with his pluck. This is a fight that at last makes the crowd count the seconds, not the money they've spent. Enough is enough, however, and the fourth round sees Castro eating canvas early on. Up he gets, and down he goes once again. The referee still doesn't put an end to the misery now being inflicted on the brave Castro, and Naz proceeds to brutalise him. He takes him down for a third and final time with 1 minute 8 seconds to go. Another win, and this time some respect is due to the challenger for his bravery.

Prince Naseem Hamed: "He was getting a bit cheeky, so I did it in four!"

53

After the hammering comes the Nazamasault!

BOTH BY PHIL COLE: ALLSPORT

SERGIO LIENDO

FIGHT 17
4 MARCH 1995

FORUM CENTRE LIVINGSTON, SCOTLAND
DEFENCE OF WBC INT.
SUPER-BANTAMWEIGHT CHAMPIONSHIP

Naz appears unconvinced about having the Argentinian flag waved over his head.

Result: That good ol' Round 2 once again!

Round 1

This is a fighter with a rep' to back up his challenge. Liendo has come to take a belt and is fast enough to cause problems. Or that's what the form book says. Rather than punch, however, it looks as if he is prepared for the long haul, moving around the ring in a defensive posture in order to draw out the Prince. Naz needs no second invitation, and steams into the man who wants his title. It takes some time, but a right nearly takes the challenger's head off, and yet more defences are put up.

Round 2

You can see that Naz wants to end this one as soon as possible. Liendo decides to try boxing, and lands punch after punch, none of which seem to worry Naseem Hamed. All they do is to annoy the hell out of him. When you poke a lion with a stick, you should be prepared for it to take your arm off. Liendo isn't and so the next piece of physical annihilation comes out of the blue, nearly putting him in the black. Naz's left-hook is incredible, shatters the Argentinian from head to legs. People gasp... yet,

Fight Statistics

REFEREE	Daniel Van de Wiele
OPPONENT	Sergio Rafael Liendo
NATIONALITY	Argentinian
AGE	25
HEIGHT	5ft 6in, 1.68m
WEIGHT	8st 10lb, 55.3kg
NAZ'S WEIGHT	8st 9lb 10oz, 55.2kg
RECORD	W41–L04–D04
HONOURS	Argentinian Super-Bantamweight Champion; South American Super-Bantamweight Champion; WBC World Super-Bantamweight Champion
RANKED	World Super-Bantamweight Number 4 (WBC)
NAZ'S PREDICTION	'I can see myself doing something inside three.'

Prince Naseem Hamed:

"When you're a professional
you should act like a pro
and a Champion"

CHRIS COLE: ALLSPORT

stunningly the referee doesn't
stop the fight. This gives Naz
the opportunity to take Liendo
down, and nearly for good, as
the challenger doesn't rise from
the canvas for nearly five
minutes after the final dreadful
punch. Naz has won, and shown
himself to be a true Champion,
albeit a merciless one.

ENRIQUE ANGELES

Prince Naseem Hamed: "I have accuracy, speed, timing, everything"

FIGHT 18
6 MAY 1995

SHEPTON MALLET LEISURE CENTRE
DEFENCE OF WBC INT. SUPER-BANTAMWEIGHT
CHAMPIONSHIP

Result: Round 2 to you Naz! KO!

Round 1
Out comes the Mexican, punching fit to bust. He looks frightening to someone slower and less inclined to bob and weave than Naz. But the punching is as much for show as anything else – Naz avoids each of the less-than-graceful attacks. Two minutes in and Naz decides to throw some back. Not only does he connect, he also draws blood with a cut to the Mexican's eye. The bell rings and both men return to their corners in very different states of body and mind.

Round 2
Get this over with. Bam! A left shocks Angeles. But after seemingly giving up all pretence at boxing, Naz backs off from the fight. He gazes over at the challenger... maybe something is wrong, maybe an old fight injury has recurred! He looks at the Mexican's boots. It's enough to put Angeles off guard. Bang! A shot to the face. Crunch! A left to the body, and the challenger goes down, not to rise again. Naz is, in his own words: 'Supreme'. There's no doubting that Angeles should have been a worthy opponent; there's no doubting he didn't stand a chance.

Both by Jogn Gichigi: Allsport

Fight Statistics

REFEREE	Larry O'Connell
OPPONENT	Enrique Angeles
NATIONALITY	Mexican
AGE	22
HEIGHT	5ft 7.5in, 1.71m
WEIGHT	8st 8lb, 54.4kg
NAZ'S WEIGHT	8st 10lb, 55.3kg
RECORD	W26–L04–D0
HONOURS	Mexican Super-Bantamweight Champion

RANKED
World Super Bantamweight Number 10 (WBA); World Super-Bantamweight Number 12 (WBF); World Super-Bantamweight Number 10 (WBU); World Super-Bantamweight Number 13 (WBC)

NAZ'S PREDICTION
None this time

Can a dazed Enrique hear angels singing? Naz doesn't give a back-toss...

'Is he really down?' The ref thinks so, and so does the Colombian, who will be nursing a broken nose on the way back to the dressing room.

JOHN GICHIGI: ALLSPORT

Fight Statistics

REFEREE
Mickey Vann-Perez

OPPONENT
Juan Polo-Perez

NATIONALITY
Colombian

AGE
31

HEIGHT
5ft 7.5in, 1.71m

WEIGHT
8st 8lb 12oz, 54.7kg

NAZ'S WEIGHT
8st 10lb, 55.3kg

RECORD
W22–L12–D02

HONOURS
IBF World Super-Flyweight Champion

RANKED
World 25 Super-Bantamweight (WBC)

NAZ'S PREDICTION
'I'm going to stop him in two.'

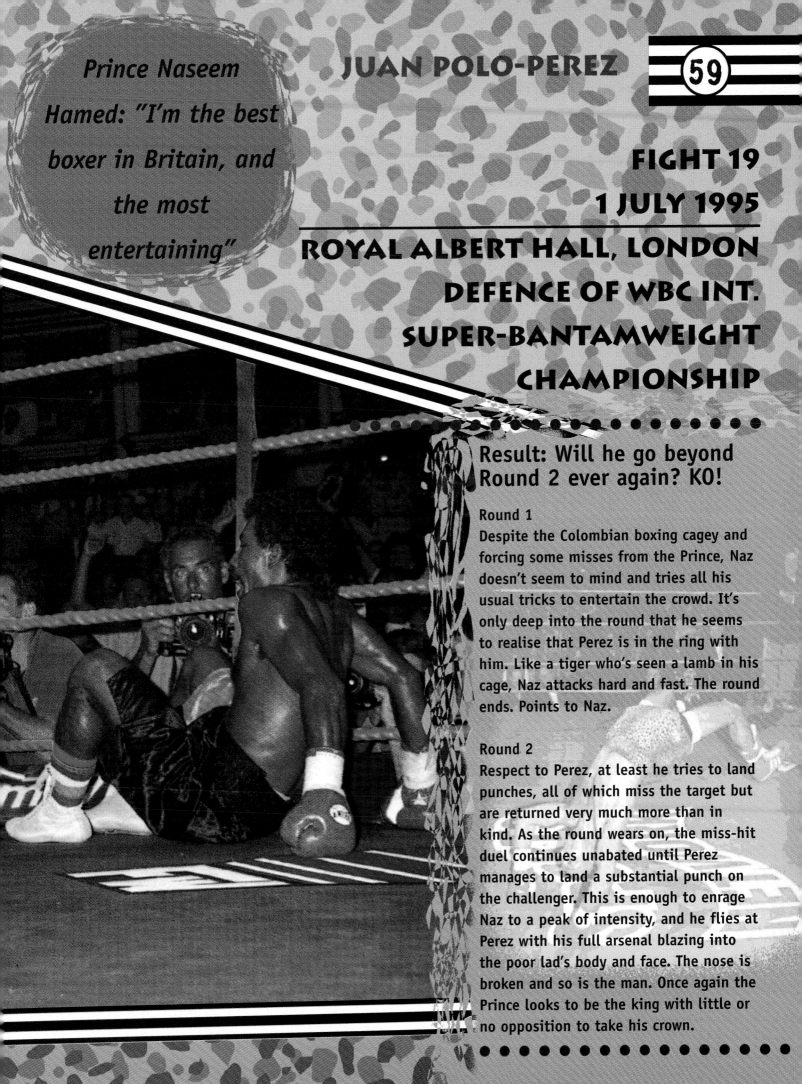

Prince Naseem Hamed: "I'm the best boxer in Britain, and the most entertaining"

JUAN POLO-PEREZ

FIGHT 19
1 JULY 1995
ROYAL ALBERT HALL, LONDON
DEFENCE OF WBC INT.
SUPER-BANTAMWEIGHT
CHAMPIONSHIP

Result: Will he go beyond Round 2 ever again? KO!

Round 1
Despite the Colombian boxing cagey and forcing some misses from the Prince, Naz doesn't seem to mind and tries all his usual tricks to entertain the crowd. It's only deep into the round that he seems to realise that Perez is in the ring with him. Like a tiger who's seen a lamb in his cage, Naz attacks hard and fast. The round ends. Points to Naz.

Round 2
Respect to Perez, at least he tries to land punches, all of which miss the target but are returned very much more than in kind. As the round wears on, the miss-hit duel continues unabated until Perez manages to land a substantial punch on the challenger. This is enough to enrage Naz to a peak of intensity, and he flies at Perez with his full arsenal blazing into the poor lad's body and face. The nose is broken and so is the man. Once again the Prince looks to be the king with little or no opposition to take his crown.

BEING THE
PUNDIT:
NAZ GETS A
CLOSE LOOK AT
HIS NEXT
OPPONENT, STEVE
ROBINSON, AS HE
COMMENTATES ON
ROBINSON'S
FIGHT AT
CARDIFF ON
4 APRIL 1995.

FIGHT 20
30 SEPTEMBER 1995
CARDIFF RUGBY FOOTBALL CLUB
WBO WORLD FEATHERWEIGHT TITLE

Result: Call the ref in Round 8! Naz the Champion!

Rounds 1–4

This is the big one. The biggest fight of his life so far. Of course it's in Wales so Naz is guaranteed of a 'warm' reception. The match build-up has ensured that there's no love lost between the two boxers either. So we're set up for a right royal rip-snorter of a bout. It's all too fast to begin with. Both fighters punch and miss but there's no doubting that the passion is there for all to see. Round Two sees Naz pushing Robinson to the floor – quite an achievement if you're unaware of Hamed's strength. Robinson had mocked this prior to the fight, so the ease with which his smaller opponent handles him comes as a shock to the Welshman and a boost to the Sheffield challenger. Round Three, and Robinson makes contact with a useful punch, which, outwardly at least (and that's all that counts), doesn't seem to worry Naz in the slightest. He's punching back, winding up both Steve Robinson – the Champion – and the heavily partisan home crowd. So far so good. Robinson is damaged around the eyes, but this doesn't stop him taking Naz through the heralded fourth round. He's far from giving up his title, in fact, despite the bruising, he looks as if he wants some more.

Fight Statistics

REFEREE	Ismael 'Wiso' Fernandez
OPPONENT	Steve Robinson
NATIONALITY	Welsh
AGE	22
HEIGHT	5ft 7.5in, 1.71m
WEIGHT	8st 13lb 12oz, 57kg
NAZ'S WEIGHT	8st 10lbs, 55.3kg
RECORD	W13–L09–D0
HONOURS	WBO World Featherweight Champion
RANKED	World Super-Bantamweight Number 10 (WBA); World Super-Bantamweight Number 12; (WBF); World Super-Bantamweight Number 10 (WBU); World Super-Bantamweight Number 13 (WBC)
NAZ'S PREDICTION	'In the Fourth.'

Robinson mocked Naz before the fight, but as the Champion found himself on the receiving end, it was the Prince's turn to do the taunting.

Rounds 5–7

Naz gets hit with a peach but retains his unconcerned stance. Robinson is without doubt the best fighter he's faced so far. Unlike Buckley, who took Hamed some distance by defensive work, Steve Robinson can, and does, box like a winner. Naz responds by offering himself to the Champion rather than backing off, and it works – the Welshman goes down for a '4!'. It's the first time he's ever smelt the canvas in his entire career. Round Six, and the Champion seems out of ideas. He's tired by the speed and elusiveness of the youngster, but like a true 'Champeen', he continues to try to hurt his foe. He lands another beauty, but this only enrages Naz, who hurricanes into him with punch after punch, to no reply. The blood is fountaining from Robinson's mouth as the round ends. Round Seven, and Naz seems more concerned with taunting the Champion than laying a glove on him. Of course the Prince is still avoiding all punches as they move into what turns into the final round.

Round 8

The World Champion's belt is in Naz's sights now as he emerges from the advice of his cornermen. Steve Robinson has landed punches. He's fought cagey and open. But he's hurt, badly hurt around the face. His body, if not his resolve, and his ability to respond are weakened. Naz knows that it's his time. Not only will taking Robinson down give the Prince the belt, it will also silence his detractors in the crowd, the assembled press, and the media world wide. This is it. He looses a huge left at Robinson's face, the Champ's own bruises obscuring his features, and Stevo goes down. Although he rises once again, the referee knows that now is the

Naz wins the WBO Featherweight Championship to round off a stunning 1995, after his successful challenge of Steve Robinson.

JOHN GICHIGI: ALLSPORT

time to stop the slaughter. He steps in. Naz leaps in delight – eyeing the ringside boxing press with disdain. But there is no disdain for Robinson. Naz, the underrated gentleman, takes the now ex-Champion's hand and raises it in a show of utmost respect. This is it. Naseem Hamed is a World Champion at 21 years of age!

Prince
Naseem Hamed:
"I'm the complete
package"

1996

Fight Statistics

REFEREE
Ismael 'Wiso' Fernandez

OPPONENT
Said Lawal

NATIONALITY
Nigerian

AGE
26

HEIGHT
5ft 5in, 1.65m

WEIGHT
8st 13lb, 56.7kg

NAZ'S WEIGHT
8st 13lb 12oz, 57kg

RECORD
W17–L01–D01

HONOURS
Austrian Featherweight Champion;
WBC World Featherweight Champion

RANKED
World Number 4 Featherweight (WBO)

NAZ'S PREDICTION
Naz didn't bother

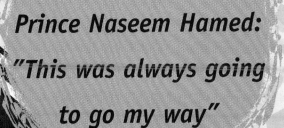

Prince Naseem Hamed: "This was always going to go my way"

FIGHT 21
16 MARCH 1996
SCOTTISH CONFERENCE CENTRE, GLASGOW
DEFENCE OF WBC INT. SUPER-BANTAMWEIGHT CHAMPIONSHIP

Result: Ouch! Round 1. No Contest!

Round 1
What do you say about a fight that lasts for 35 seconds? Lawal has never fought outside of his adopted home in Austria, he is older but not wiser than Naz. And he hits the deck with less than a half minute gone. Okay, so Naz punches him to the floor in less than four seconds, the Prince must be wondering what he's doing here wasting his time. Then, 31 seconds later, Lawal is down and very, very out indeed. There's no competition. Naz has destroyed him utterly. Time to move on.

TRAINING FOR THE STRENUOUS YEAR AHEAD: LOOKING GOOD IN FRONT OF THE MIRROR IS ALL IMPORTANT...

ANTON WANT: ALLSPORT

...JUST AS IMPORTANT AS LOOKING MEAN AND MOODY FOR THE CAMERAMEN... IT'S ALL A QUESTION OF

JOHN GICHIGI: ALLSPORT

GETTING THE POSE RIGHT, AS NAZ PREPARES TO TAKE ON DANIEL ALICEA TO DEFEND HIS WBO FEATHERWEIGHT CHAMPIONSHIP TITLE IN NEWCASTLE.

DANIEL ALICEA

FIGHT 22

8 JUNE 1996

NEWCASTLE ARENA

DEFENCE OF WBO

FEATHERWEIGHT

CHAMPIONSHIP

Result: Naz goes down but comes up to win in 2!

Round 1

Who knew? Who could have guessed that a fighter like the unrated 'Pipino' would be the first man to put Naz to the deck? The Prince is certainly unaware of this potential, and so when the punch comes that takes his legs from beneath him, yet another lesson is brutally learnt. It's apparent from the look in Alicea's eyes that he is stunned by his own achievement. Is this the end for the arrogant 'king in waiting'? As all the critics had been suggesting for months, would his first taste of the floor really show him up for the Clown Prince that they are all so certain he is?

Round 2

The guys from Adidas must be weeping in their chequebooks at the first round action. They've just signed Naz to a huge sponsorship deal – could this have cursed him? Please! The sign of a true Champion, from Marciano through Ali to Leonard is that he performs in the ring no matter what. He gets up and fights back. If you don't do this, you're simply a brawler. Brendan has trained Naz for this eventuality, he's a realist and so is Naz. So when the Prince bounces back into the ring and hands out a right-left combination to put Alicea firmly in his place – out for the count – no one in the Prince's

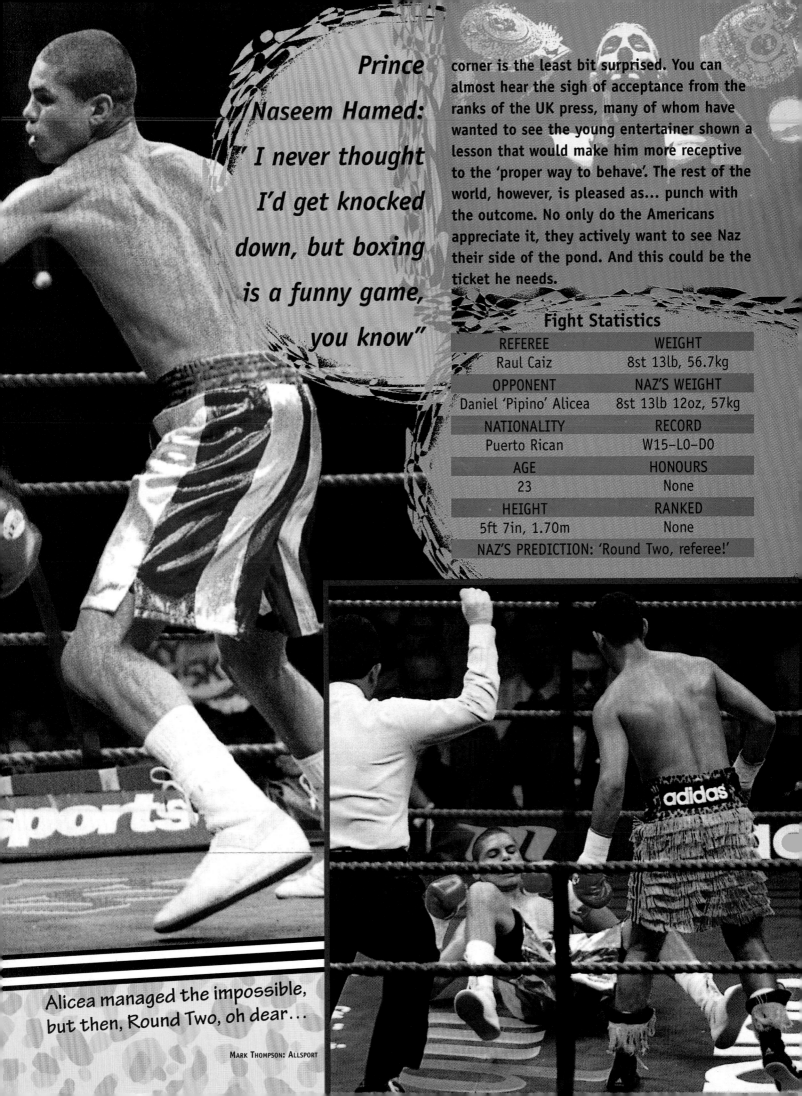

Prince Naseem Hamed: *"I never thought I'd get knocked down, but boxing is a funny game, you know"*

corner is the least bit surprised. You can almost hear the sigh of acceptance from the ranks of the UK press, many of whom have wanted to see the young entertainer shown a lesson that would make him more receptive to the 'proper way to behave'. The rest of the world, however, is pleased as... punch with the outcome. No only do the Americans appreciate it, they actively want to see Naz their side of the pond. And this could be the ticket he needs.

Fight Statistics

REFEREE	**WEIGHT**
Raul Caiz	8st 13lb, 56.7kg
OPPONENT	**NAZ'S WEIGHT**
Daniel 'Pipino' Alicea	8st 13lb 12oz, 57kg
NATIONALITY	**RECORD**
Puerto Rican	W15–L0–D0
AGE	**HONOURS**
23	None
HEIGHT	**RANKED**
5ft 7in, 1.70m	None
NAZ'S PREDICTION: 'Round Two, referee!'	

Alicea managed the impossible, but then, Round Two, oh dear…

IT'S A DIFFERENT
SORT OF CATWALK
FOR THE NEW PRINCE
OF FASHION:
NAZ POSES FOR A
SPORSTWEAR
LAUNCH IN LONDON
16 MAY 1996.

"My favourite clothes have designer labels... I just love shopping for new gear"

JUAN MEDINA

FIGHT 23

31 AUGUST 1996

THE POINT, DUBLIN

DEFENCE OF WBO FEATHERWEIGHT CHAMPIONSHIP

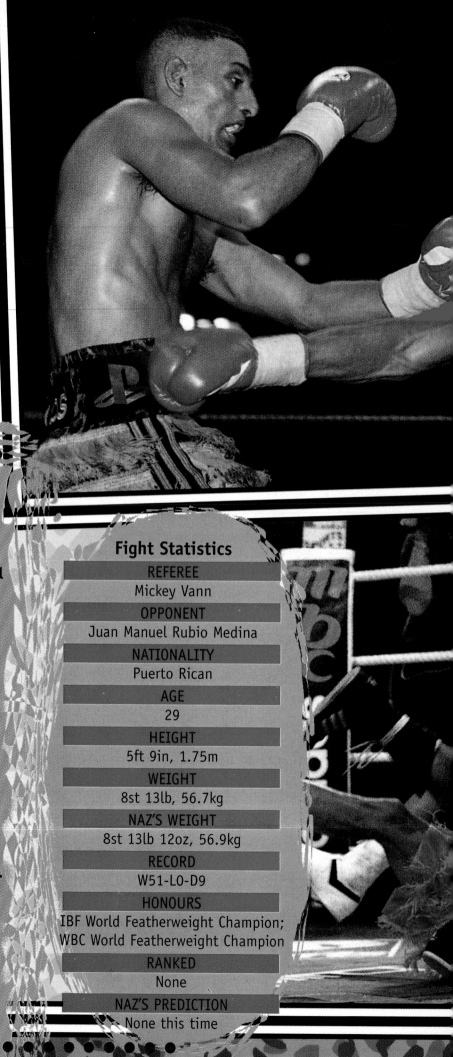

Result: 11 Rounds of punishment, but still a win!

Rounds 1–6

Naz knows he's up against some severe competition in Medina, a real fighter who will definitely offer resistance. The Puerto Rican has held World belts, has not been stopped inside the distance in the last seven years, and is young and agile enough to contend with Naz's speed. In the first round they check each other out – perhaps the infection Naz picked up is holding him back, but the first round passes with little or no incident. Round Two opens with Naz finding some weakness in his foe's tight defence – he manages to take the former world champion down! But Medina isn't a fighter to go out in the fateful second round, and he's up again, apparently unshattered physically or mentally. Rounds Three, Four, Five and Six are a nightmare for Naseem.

The crowd is turning against him, and he can almost hear a joyful English media contingent scratching his boxing obituary as he fights. Again and again his defence is breached as punches from Medina find their

Fight Statistics

REFEREE	
Mickey Vann	
OPPONENT	
Juan Manuel Rubio Medina	
NATIONALITY	
Puerto Rican	
AGE	
29	
HEIGHT	
5ft 9in, 1.75m	
WEIGHT	
8st 13lb, 56.7kg	
NAZ'S WEIGHT	
8st 13lb 12oz, 56.9kg	
RECORD	
W51-L0-D9	
HONOURS	
IBF World Featherweight Champion; WBC World Featherweight Champion	
RANKED	
None	
NAZ'S PREDICTION	
None this time	

Prince Naseem Hamed:
"Manuel Medina is a great fighter and I took him"

way through. This is possibly the first real defence that Naz has had to put up, and he's not reacting well. For four rounds the challenger finds gaps and exploits them. Naz attempts to show-boat in order to escape, but this only enrages the crowd further. Naz suddenly looks very alone, almost vulnerable, as they move into the seventh.

Rounds 7–11
Whatever Brendan has whispered in his ear as he sits surveying his options in between the rounds must have worked. Naz comes into the seventh with the task of making back some points or at least reaching an in-ring parity. He starts repairing the damage by tightening his guard and manages to land a few punches. This hard labour bears fruit in the eighth, and some of the old confidence comes seeping back. Coming out for the ninth, all of a sudden the gaps in Medina's guard become blindingly obvious and Naz puts him down with a tremendous right 40 seconds into the round. Barely 25 seconds later a combination knocks out Medina's lights. But the lights come on again in time to take the next two rounds to some kind of equality. However, by sheer damage Medina is far worse off. His face is a mess, his eyes are cut, and Naz is now moving too fast for the Puerto Rican's blood-blurred vision. The crowd, for some reason, shout their disapproval when the referee moves in to stop the bout at the end of Round 11. It has been the best challenge the Sheffield world beater has yet faced, and he's effusive in his praise for Medina in the press conference. But not so fulsome as to leave anyone in any doubt about who really is the champion of the world. Surely America must be soon!

With the lethal speed and aggressiveness of a velociraptor, Naz stands poised over his felled opponent – Medina is finished.

Fight Statistics

REFEREE
Roberto Ramirez

OPPONENT
Remigio Daniel Molina Ferreyra

NATIONALITY
Argentinian

AGE
27

HEIGHT
5ft 9in, 1.75m

WEIGHT
8st 13lb, 56.7kg

NAZ'S WEIGHT
8st 13lb 12oz, 57kg

RECORD
W28–L0–D0

HONOURS
None

RANKED
None

NAZ'S PREDICTION
None this time

REMIGIO MOLINA

Prince Naseem Hamed: "I'm probably the hardest-punching featherweight ever"

FIGHT 24
9 NOVEMBER 1996
MANCHESTER NYNEX ARENA
DEFENCE OF WBO FEATHERWEIGHT
CHAMPIONSHIP

BOTH BY JOHN GICHIGI: ALLSPORT

Result: Back on form with a Round 2 KO!

Round 1
Remigio Molina, has come to teach Naz a few lessons at the Manchester Nynex in an attempt to take the belt. It's been a hard but productive year for the Prince, could this be one fight too many? No way. He emerges from his corner ready and willing to do the business. Showing his usual range of tricks, and using both the orthodox and southpaw stances, he deluges the Argentinian with combinations and straight punches to the body. Molina's last battle had been a decision win over ten rounds. He's unbeaten in 28 bouts, but this seems to show for little or nothing. Naz is too quick.

Round 2
The second round is traditionally Naz's happy hunting ground and this time is no different. He dances out of his corner with one thought in mind, getting behind that guard and taking his man to the canvas. It's not long before the challenger is reeling from a set of blows, lefts and rights, that shatter any composure he has left. Naz plays to the crowd and mocks Molina at the same time. Two rounds of this kind of abuse are enough and, with time left to tick, Molina is in no fit state to continue. The referee is forced to intervene, and that's it. Job done. End of chat. Naz finishes the year as he intended – a World Champion.

77

**3 FEBRUARY:
NAZ SHOWS THE
PRESS HIS FAST
NEW CAR FOR A
SPEEDY BOXER**

N4 NAS

MARK THOMPSON: ALLSPORT

FIGHT 25
8 FEBRUARY 1997
LONDON ARENA
UNIFICATION OF WBO AND IBF

Result: All done and unified in eight rounds!

Rounds 1–4

This fight will provide Naz with more than money, it will swell him with the kind of glory that very few boxers in history can attain. Unifying the belts of two boxing boards will be an achievement that might just silence some of the critics. Johnson has an excellent record and is a worthy opponent. Naz is faster, much much faster, however, and he uses this to bemuse the bigger man. But for once a Prince opponent is returning fire and getting closer than others who preceded him. Round Three is the beginning of the end for 'Boom Boom', though, as Naz stuns him with a tremendous combination. To his credit, Johnson remains on his feet and boxing. And what boxing: stunning Naz, who isn't used to getting what he gives, the American lands a huge right-hand. This is not going to be plain sailing, even if the Sheffield fighter looks superior in every aspect of the art.

Everything looks pally enough at the pre-fight press conference, but Tom 'Boom Boom' Johnson is about to give Naz the third really really long battle of his career.

MARK THOMPSON: ALLSPORT

Prince Naseem Hamed: "I tried watching him ['Boom Boom'] on video but after about two rounds I got bored"

Fight Statistics

REFEREE	Rudy Battle
OPPONENT	Tom "Boom Boom" Johnson
NATIONALITY	American
AGE	32
HEIGHT	5ft 5in, 1.65m
WEIGHT	8st 5lb, 53.1kg
NAZ'S WEIGHT	8st 5lb 12oz, 53.4kg
RECORD	W44–L2–D2
HONOURS	IBF Featherweight World Champion
RANKED	World Number 1 (WBU); World Number 1 (IBF); World Number 4 (IBO); World Number 4 (WBB)
NAZ'S PREDICTION	'In the third round... baby!!'

MAIN BY JOHN GICHIGI, INSET BY MARK THOMPSON: ALLSPORT

Rounds 4–8

On and on they box with the possibility of the full 12 rounds looming ever larger in the minds of both men. This is a real challenge for Naseem, it should make the press take notice of his skill, speed and ability to learn as he fights. Despite catching some fists from Johnson, it looks as if Naz understands his enemy better as every second passes. Moving smoothly from fourth through to eight, handing out and taking punishment, the look in Naz's eye is steely shark-like. By the eighth he knows where the weakness lies and is ready to exploit it. This he does with a brain-blistering right uppercut, which puts Johnson out on the deck. The referee begins the count, Naz stands preparing to floor Johnson if he even thinks about rising from his prone position. Nothing of the sort happens, as 'Boom Boom' is counted as down and very much out. Naz is the Champion!

FIGHT 26
3 MAY 1997
MANCHESTER NYNEX
DEFENCE OF WBO AND
IBF FEATHERWEIGHT TITLES

Is that three rounds, two or one, or even a fat zero rounds, Naz is counting against Billy Hardy before their featherweight fist match? As it turned out , the Prince's prediction was spot on.

BARRY M PRIOR: ALLSPORT

Billy Hardy:

"He's going to be the four-time World Champion because he's got that knockout punch"

The Prince prepares for a short bout.

MARK THOMPSON: ALLSPORT

Result: Why take it too far when you can do it in the first? KO!

Round 1

93 seconds. The punch, the first real punch of the bout, goes in hard from the right hand and sends Hardy to the mat for the count of '7!'. He rises, groggy and not sure where (or why?) he's here at all. But he's not up for long, as a combination from Naz, finishing with a brutal left, sends Hardy over once again. The count is '6!' but, while Hardy rises for more, it's been enough for the referee, who puts a stop to the battle.

Fight Statistics

REFEREE
Paul Thomas

OPPONENT
Billy Hardy

NATIONALITY
English

AGE
32

HEIGHT
5ft 6in, 1.68m

WEIGHT
8st 5lb, 53.1kg

NAZ'S WEIGHT
8st 5lb 12oz, 53.4kg

RECORD
W36–L7–D2

HONOURS
Great Britain Bantamweight; Commonwealth
Featherweight; Great Britain Featherweight;
European Featherweight

RANKED
WBC 3rd IBF 11th

NAZ'S PREDICTION
'Inside the first!'

'Sorry, Billy, what was that you said about going the distance?'

The first round has barely warmed up and Hardy's down for a second time, this one for a '6'. It's enough for the ref… cue a victorious Nazamasault.

MAIN PICTURE AND TWO LOWER INSETS BY JOHN GICHIGI;
UPPER INSET BY MARK THOMPSON: ALLSPORT

JUAN CABRERA

FIGHT 27
19 JULY 1997

WEMBLEY ARENA
DEFENCE OF WBO AND IBF
FEATHERWEIGHT TITLES

Result: Magic Round 2. KO!

Round 1

Cabrera isn't even supposed to be here. He's an eleventh hour replacement for fellow Argentinian Pastor Martin, who picked up an eye injury while sparring the previous week. That said, his record is impressive and should, if he comes out punching, give Naz a run for his very substantial money. Sadly for fight fans, and for the Prince's growing reputation – which can only really flourish if he faces good opposition – Cabrera prefers the cagey approach. Naz, of course, punches his way through that defence, leaving the Argentinian white-faced with shock on his return to the corner.

Round 2

It's as if Naz has had quite enough of the punchless foe, as he steams in using his full arsenal, plus a few of his usual antics. Yet again, offering himself up with a dropped guard and wandering eyes can't draw the other fighter out. So Naz goes for the big style – a right uppercut and a crushing left-hand seem to remove all power from Cabrera's legs. Naz goes in so hard, in fact, that the referee has to stop the bout with 2 minutes and 17 seconds gone in the round.

It always starts with smiles... then comes the dodging and the running.

ABOVE BY MARK THOMPSON; BELOW AND RIGHT BY JOHN GICHIGI: Allsport

Fight Statistics

REFEREE
Lou Moret

OPPONENT
Juan Gerardo Cabrera

NATIONALITY
Argentinian

AGE
22

HEIGHT
5ft 6in, 1.68m

WEIGHT
8st 5lb, 53.1kg

NAZ'S WEIGHT
8st 5lb 12oz, 53.4kg

RECORD
W24–L02–D0

HONOURS
None

RANKED
World Number 7 (WBO)

NAZ'S PREDICTION
'...he says he's going to knock me out in six. I predict I'll knock him out in two.'

Prince Naseem Hamed:
"...now the Americans know the best featherweight in the world is from Sheffield, England"

26 JUNE 1997

NEW YORK, USA

Naz models for Adidas in New York.
Madison Square's over that
way, Naseem…

BOTH BY AL BELLO: ALLSPORT

Jay Larkin,

senior vice-president

of cable network ShowTime:

"Naz is not as well known in

America as he should be.

If we can do a deal for his

next fight he could top

the bill in the States."

Madison Square Gardens has to be one of the world's supreme boxing venues, not so much for its facilities, more for its long association with flying sweat under the hot spotlights as fist meets flesh and bone. So when Naseem visited New York for a sportswear fashion shoot shortly before his defeat of Cabrera, he was as close to the heart of his ambition for a New York fight as he had been all his professional career.

Standing on the New Jersey shoreline, staring out across the Hudson river at the towers of lower Manhattan, the young fighter could only hope that soon, someone would have the courage to answer promoter Frank Warren's continual offers for a match.

In the meantime, there were a few hours ahead in the location make-up cabin to prepare for the long night's photo shoot... time enough to dream of a victorious return to the US, possibly in 1998.

PRINCE NASEEM

A YET BRIEF CAREER IN BRIEF

From a frighteningly early age, Naseem Hamed was an achiever, and here for quick reference is his form so far...

AMATEUR CAREER

Fought: 67
Won: 62
Lost: 5 (all of these on points)

Amateur Record and Titles

1987	National Schools Junior Champion 32kg class
1989	National Schools Intermediate Champion 42kg class
1989	England Schools versus Wales, won two bouts
1990	National Association of Boys Clubs Class 'A' Champion 48kg class
1990	National Schools Senior Champion 48kg class
1990	Junior Amateur Boxing Association Class 'B' Champion 48kg class

Vital Statistics

FULL NAME
Naseem Salom Ali Hamed

DATE OF BIRTH
12 February 1974

HEIGHT
5ft 3in, 1.60m

FIGHTING WEIGHT
8st 10lb–9st, 55.3–57kg

WALK AROUND WEIGHT
9st 2lb–9st 6lb, 58–60kg

CHEST
36in, 91.5cm

REACH
63in, 1.60m

WAIST
29in, 73.6cm

THIGH
29in, 73.6cm

FIST
10in, 25.5cm

RECORD
F27–W27–L0–D0

1990 England Youth squad versus US Junior Olympic squad, won one bout against Dan Acevedo

1991 Junior Amateur Boxing Association Class 'B' Champion 51kg class

1991 National Association of Boys Clubs Class 'C' Champion 51kg class

1991 England Under 19 team – trip to Tunisia was called off

PROFESSIONAL CAREER

Naz's career up to and including his fight with Juan Cabrera July 19, 1997 reads like someone who can't count to two – he's won everything with only the slightest of upsets along the way. His statistics stand as 27–27–0–0: fought 27, won 27, lost none, drawn none and in brief they read as follows:

Date	Opponent	Result	Method	Round	Venue
1992					
April 14	Ricky Beard	W	KO	2	Mansfield, England
April 25	Shaun Norman	W	TKO	2	Manchester, England
May 23	Andrew Bloomer	W	TKO	2	Birmingham, England
July14	Miguel Matthews	W	TKO	3	Mayfair, London, England
October 7	Des Gargano	W	TKO	4	Sunderland, England
November 12	Peter Buckley	W	Points	6	Liverpool, England
1993					
February 24	Alan Ley	W	KO	2	Wembley, England
May 26	Kevin Jenkins	W	TKO	3	Mansfield, England
September 24	Chris Clarkson	W	KO	2	Dublin, Eire
1994					
January 29	Peter Buckley	W	TKO	4	Cardiff, Wales
April 12	John Miceli	W	KO	1	Mansfield, England

May 11

European Bantamweight Title Challenge

	Vincenzo Belcastro	W	Points	12	Sheffield, England

August 17

Defence of European Bantamweight Championship

	Antonio Picardi	W	TKO	3	Sheffield, England

October 12

Vacant WBC Int. Super-Bantamweight Championship

	Freddy Cruz	W	TKO	6	Sheffield, England

November 19

Defence of WBC Int. Super-Bantamweight Championship

	Laureano Ramirez	W	TKO	3	Cardiff, Wales

1995

January 21

Defence of WBC Int. Super-Bantamweight Championship

	Armando Castro	W	TKO	4	Glasgow, Scotland

Date	Opponent	Result	Method	Round	Venue

March 4

Defence of WBC Int. Super-Bantamweight Championship

	Sergio Rafael Liendo	W	KO	2	Livingston, Scotland

May 6

Defence of WBC Int. Super-Bantamweight Championship

	Enrique Angeles	W	KO	2	Shepton Mallet, England

July 1

Defence of WBC Int. Super-Bantamweight Championship

	Juan Polo-Perez	W	KO	2	Kensington, London, England

September 30

Challenge for WBO Featherweight Championship

	Steve Robinson	W	KO	8	Cardiff, Wales

1996

March 16

Defence of WBO Featherweight Championship

	Said Lawal	W	KO	1	Glasgow, Scotland

June 8

Defence of WBO Featherweight Championship

	Daniel Alicea	W	KO	3	Newcastle, England

August 31

Defence of WBO Featherweight Championship

	Manuel Medina	W	TKO	11	Dublin, Eire

November 9

Defence of WBO Featherweight Championship

	Remigio Molina	W	TKO	2	Manchester, England

1997

February 8

Unification of WBO and IBF Featherweight Titles

IBF Champion

	Tom Johnson	W	TKO	8	London, England

May 3

Defence of WBO and IBF Featherweight titles

	Billy Hardy	W	KO	1	Manchester, England

July 19

Defence of WBO and IBF Featherweight titles

	Juan Cabrera	W	KO	2	London, England

Pensive Naz –
there's a lot more
of the story to
follow . . . . . .